As
Water
is to
Seed

As *Water* is to *Seed*

J. QUENTIN BROWN

iUniverse®

AS WATER IS TO SEED

iUniverse books may be ordered through booksellers or by contacting:

iUniverse
1663 Liberty Drive
Bloomington, IN 47403
www.iuniverse.com
1-800-Authors (1-800-288-4677)

Because of the dynamic nature of the Internet, any web addresses or links contained in this book may have changed since publication and may no longer be valid. The views expressed in this work are solely those of the author and do not necessarily reflect the views of the publisher, and the publisher hereby disclaims any responsibility for them.

Any people depicted in stock imagery provided by Getty Images are models, and such images are being used for illustrative purposes only. Certain stock imagery © Getty Images.

ISBN: 978-1-5320-8374-7 (sc)
ISBN: 978-1-5320-8375-4 (e)

Print information available on the last page.

iUniverse rev. date: 09/27/2019

BOOK I

Heart Seed

Just Between Us

In all the ocean's divergence
a single possibility exists
This torrid sea
churned by incessant storm
to a caldron of passion
claws at the mantle
rears from terra-firma
It is a destructive force
self-chastising
all consuming
It is love
        between
           us

When Love Is Like The Sea

There are times
when love is like the Earth
solid and firm
secure
There are times when
love is like the sky
bright, light and breezy
More often than not
I have found
love is like the sea
coursing, ebbing, swelling
only to pull away
after seething climax
to roll, slither and run
shrinking
Into itself

Love I

to gaze into her sparkling eyes
there on a beach beneath blue skies

to touch her face, hold her hand
or build a castle in the sand

to walk beside her by the sea
these moments she has given me

Love III

Come, my love
And we will walk hand-in-hand
Down the road of insecurity
Laughing
Come, my ecstasy
And we will travel to hillsides
Of sun-ripened beauty
Come, my necessity
And we will sit beneath the tree
Of hopes and dreams
Come, my desire
And we will share our knowledge
Each with that of the other
Come, my love
And we will thrive
in this world together

Love IV

I hope you know I love you
that
you are my strength
my reason for being
what little I am
As much as I shall be
and
I hope you know I need you

Winter Hue

Only the blacks and grays
on the canvas white
color winter's days
shaping sparkling light

Gone the greens and blues
seen in warmer times
Gone the varied hues
Autumn's gay designs

Somber moods have come
on the chilling wind
pushing us toward home
and the warmth within

When winter's white
covers over our track
brightening the night
dappling gray and black

That is when I see
against this tableau
splash the shades of me
and the color — you

Love V

I cannot love
the fleeting kiss
of one who smiles
and walks away

It pains to know
I'm one in line
waiting my turn
to give you joy

Your standard shall
become my own
the two the same
when next we meet

and then, a while
I'll spare the pain
we do not share
next time you go

My Heart

Who, my heart, could teach me
to love the rolling sea
to love the square rigged ships
the water's silent slip?
Yes
my heart
it is thee

As sun now sets to lea
I sail the lonely sea
upon my captain's ship
before the wind's fair nip
and where
my heart
where are thee?

A Truer Love

there is a girl so pretty
I do dare too much to love
an angel in uniform
a waitress with golden hair
yet there is more gold to see
the ring shows she's spoken for

I guess I could best love her
by hiding my desire
she would never have to know
the pain of an adultery
and she will be as happy
as I could ever make her

The D. T. Sheridan

The deeply rusted hull
of the D. T. Sheridan
lies on its mutilated side
upon the boulder beach
looking,
as if rejected from its home
over the living, breathing ocean

The tug's crew
was once of strong men
sweating and straining
in their tiresome task
The Washerwoman watched the transition
during a night when work was hardest
Gull Rock loomed near-by
behind a shroud of slashing rain
The fog bell's clang-clang
clang-clang
an unheard dirge
for the wind and waves

Now the only passengers are lovers
of beauty
of solitude
of one another
sitting silently
legs swinging lightly from the keel

The ebbing tide
threatens dreaming lovers
Foaming swaths
rush over rounded rocks
reaching
wave-by-wave
beneath the hulk
driving the passionate
again
from their vigil
The ocean seeming to reclaim
Its long lost booty

BOOK II

Mind Seed

Writers Block

poets of your time come
do gather around my bed
I think my best part gone
the mind is surely dead
fast going all the rest
I call on you, dear friends
your words to cure me best
and waive my feared sad ends

Lazy Layabout

I'm nothing but
a lazy lout
with naught to do
but lay about
and count the stars
within the sky
and wait for dawn
to greet my eye

Hope

Yet
when death and pain are all about
in dark and dank decaying doubt
a match may strike and flare up bright
the match that might
a candle light
and help, in turn, to light the lamp
that sheds way the dark and damp
that prods our souls and minds awake
guides our way to the day-break

Time

Time, time
For no man waits
It plods along
through hours and dates
a moment lost
can never more
be lost or found
thus I implore
spare you the grief
of an unlived lifetime

LoveLust

It began long ago
when the Earth first quaked within me

From that whispered pulse it grew
ever outward from the heart
becoming soon
a soul consuming molten flow
encompassing all that is necessary
            in the Universe

From time to time
the tumult may quiet
yet never does it cease
with tremors as intense
those vibrations move me still

Throbbing
in the endless cycles of time

From This Earth

As from the earth
we come at birth
to let sunshine
nourish our day

back to the earth
we go in death
to let the rain
erode away

the dust of our creation

House Abandoned

I stand here at the door
hand poised to ring the bell
as if it were before
the house became a shell

No one to say, "Come in
so glad to see you home"
Gram had gone to heaven
and Grampa died alone

Pushing through the doorway
peering 'round the kitchen
a distant yesterday
blurred the empty vision

Linoleum so sad
lay on the oaken floor
its pattern faded bad
with cracks from door to door

Gone the table, stool and chair
stove that Gram had tended
Gone, too, the Frigidaire
Wood box lay up-ended

Bare cupboards on the wall
make pantry feel the same

A mattress in the hall
lay bent as if in shame

The living room, to me
when last I stood in there
so near the Christmas tree
had over-filled with cheer

Women set the tables
while children played with toys
and men told their tales
this house fair shook with noise

Now only August breath
stirs dust through broken pane
as if some horrid death
inhabits pore and grain

This house, with speed, I flee
afar to watch it from
beneath the apple tree
my heart beats like a drum

It stands for all the world
an empty locust skin
The clapboard siding curled
and paintless, rotting thin

I'd come in hopes to find
a glimpse of times gone by
But mem'rys in the mind
Live on while houses die

Brave Day

Brazen is the moment
that scoffs the doubts and fears of night
and greets the bitterness of dawn
with a hearty laugh
and warms the day
with a smile

Now

Yesterday I came
tomorrow I must go
but today I am all here

The Tree On The Hill

The tree upon the hill
it looked so sad that day
The wind did blow so shrill
The sky so cold and gray

Since food I'd had my fill
and heat I felt all day
I sought to bend God's will
when knelt at bed to pray

"My dad pays every bill
Mom helps me every day
but tree upon the hill
is in a poorly way

"Please send him, if you will
my red plaid coat," I pray
"to keep off winter's chill
and maybe one sun ray

"I know its in your skill
Amen for now, okay
and go to bed I will
so quick, without delay"

I slept that night so still
'till sun lit where I lay
then jumped to window sill
and pulled the shade away

Out there the wind was nil
and sun so bright, hurray
Much snow lay on the hill
The tree stood on display

It wore a coat and frill
so thick and white, I'd say
its heart with joy must thrill
to keep the cold at bay

Then I in pj's still
ran down the fastest way
to check my stocking's fill
and gifts on Christmas Day

This I Ask

You I hang, oh wreath, upon my door
and bid of you as I bid before
to show the world in the light of day
by dark of night or the snowstorm gray
that Christmas Spirit does here-in stay

Greet them all, oh wreath upon my door
and welcome strangers as friends e'er more
to share the warmth of our hearth homey
for we are one in this family
the boughs and branches on life's tall tree

What we give, oh wreath upon my door
is hope to those either pained or poor
To them we open our Ingleside
So raise the cup to the bright yuletide
and praise that life within us resides

This I ask, oh wreath upon my door

The Homeland

Think of stepping on shore and finding it Heaven
of taking hold of a hand and finding it God's hand
of breathing a new air and finding it celestial air
of feeling invigorated and finding it immortality
of passing from storm and tempest to an unbroken calm
of waking up and finding yourself Home

The Ship Of Dream

Last night a dream sailed up to me
It drifted out of dreadful dark
within a winged and traveled bark
upon a low, unruffled sea

I found myself in paradise
an isle where time had just begun
where youth could swell in warming sun
and life was seen through laughing eyes

The fresh, blue, nearly cloudless sky
and cool sea breeze were keeping me
so light of heart and flying free
that I, its truth, did not deny

But fleeting night became the day
that drove the ship away from shore
My mind awoke, to dream no more
of diamond isle and sandy bay

'Though sleep comes harder than before
and dreams of youth less frequently
I wait beside the restless sea
to sail that ship of dream once more

Hectic Season

Why all the holiday shopping
present wrapping, tagging, sending
the busy crowds, the push and shove
why spend so much on those we love

In the grip of hectic shopping
snow-bound traffic, party hopping
it's hard to keep our goal in mind
the common gift we hope to find

Amid Christmas' rush and glitter
we should pause to reconsider
and think of what we most wish for
in very midst of season's chore

If we could choose a gift unique
one even Santa could not beat
that gift is surely peace of mind
and happiness for all in kind

BOOK III

Body Seed

An Overdue Homecoming

Its been so long
so (too long) last
at home I am again
among my friends
in forest thick
forever to remain

I know them all
as relatives
(by sight if not by name)
I wonder how
I ever left
the world from which I came

The trees still stand
upon the ground
so tall and stern and proud
Delicate moss
cover their dead
with soft and greenish shroud

The birds converse
quite cheerfully
not minding that I hear
The grass is sparse
yet cringes not
whenever I step near

The stream offers
a boulder seat
and to my feet caress
The wind and sun
exclude me not
from their soothing essence

The deer regard
me shyly now
for so much time has passed
But this is home
and I am back
at long, long (too long) last

The Trail Ahead

Trembling
I turn the bend
in a trail
monotonously long and hard
Anxious to know
I peek through branches and brush
for a glimpse
of what might lie ahead
Its not until
the way straightens
that I see
the brightness beyond
Though not suddenly easier
I proceed with lighter heart
and hopes
of better things to come

I Take The River's Way

From the mountainsides
dressed in green forests
and fields of tall grass
the stream flows happily downward
over pebbly brook bottoms
and rocky river beds
to rest, finally, in the sea

The river runs
between the hills calling from cliffs
and large boulders
crossing lakes
with little effort
always taking the easiest route
to rest, finally, in the sea

I have become as the river
taking the path of least resistance
to rest, finally, where I may

Babbling Brook

The babbling brook
brings weary winter
warmth
A lazy land
laden yet with the burden
of banks and patches
of crystal crusted snow
diminished daily
by wind and rain
melting in meadows
sodden under step
and on hills hidden
by forest flanks
quiet and questioning
waits, wanton
for the lush
leaves of green and growing
to decorate the daring
dancing shimmering stream's
bending, brimming banks

In The Company Of Solitude

I rested awhile in my labor
sitting on the pile of four-foot lengths
and looked, then, at the blue-gray shadows
of uncut trees fast growing over
                              yellow-orange white
I listened to the breath of winter
cold wind in birch twigs and cedar boughs
hearing around me the quiet hush
pervading the aging day, muted
                              absorbed in snow
I returned to my tiresome task
neither alone nor an intruder
in the company of solitude
I am but one of the family
                              hoping to survive

Respect

As into the face of Nature you stare
You learn who you are and why you are there
Constant reminder — the weight of the pack
With all that you need tightly to your back
Weary, callused feet and thin-worn boot soles
They that know the miles speak loudly your goals
Deep night's sleep after the toil of day
Teach you a respect for Nature's way

The Evening Sea

The ocean is as calm
as ever I have seen
a shallow surf along
the shore, and nothing more

Poised clouds of many shapes
the dusk's last rays do catch
casting wan reflections
to anxious, grasping earth

Alone and still once more
the evening sea can rest
The toil of day now done
the dark of night may come

Futures

I walk this road
this wooded road
a life blessed with sunshine

Around each bend
beyond each rise
wait many an unlived Life-time

Narrow Trail

The air
against the sky feels
as though
it could ring
against the ear
and blows
across barren land
to make the life
of a lonely man
an even harder trail
in this place of fewer towns
than game
to hunt
and more miles
between them
than a man has whiskers
to protect his face
from the short winter days
and cold, bitter nights
when crystalline-white bed sheets
are more often changed
by the restless wind
than gray clouds decide the sterile tundra
needs a fresh linen cover
to remind the isolated inhabitant
that his unkindly world

is rather a friend
to he who must reap sustenance
along
the thin foot-trail
and knows by what means he
survives

The Ship Of Dream

Last night a dream sailed up to me
It drifted out of dreadful dark
within a winged and traveled bark
upon a low, unruffled sea

I found myself in paradise
an isle where time had just begun
where youth could swell in warming sun
and life was seen through laughing eyes

The fresh, blue, nearly cloudless sky
and cool sea breeze were keeping me
so light of heart and flying free
that I, its truth, did not deny

But fleeting night became the day
that drove the ship away from shore
My mind awoke, to dream no more
of diamond isle and sandy bay

'Though sleep comes harder than before
and dreams of youth less frequently
I wait beside the restless sea
to sail that ship of dream once more

River's Cycle

The river is born on the mountain
Conceived at the peak
where the rain's mass is cleaved
covering rock and soil
mere wetness
Formless and with no more direction than down
It gathers into rills and gullies
From this point
to the ocean
the river's course is confined
defined
by reaction with its environment

The infant stream speaks softly its first few words
babbling as it bubbles, bounces
skitters, swirls and shoots
among rocks passing underfoot
Through waxing ages of youth the stream's voice deepens
The stronger body
runs, cascades and plays
more loudly
for youth is mighty
Youth is majestic

Youth is momentary
Maturity is certain

excitement giving way to efficiency
The river compromises
between speed and effort
The stream cares less for the thrill
of long falls and sharp bends
taking them more easily
content with a retiring, wandering course

The ocean is not far off now
The river is not anxious
to leave its comfortable bed
the way meandering aimlessly
its motion slow
as if to consume time
to delay the inevitable fate
So creeps old age

The river does not die
Its form is lost
dispersed into the ocean
but its waters flow on
beside the souls of many rivers
on, around the planet
waiting to be drawn up
waiting to be reborn

Descent

Amid the colors
deep of hue
and light reflected crystal flash
worn by tread of boot
the trail takes me down
worn out legs placing tired feet
one step more
one ledge at a time
done the hardest part
topping out
to infinite view
behind now
an anti-climax
Camp awaits below
R-and-R
The warmth of summer's
setting sun
and the gift of rest

Retirement

Upon the shelf
empty they stand
laces knotted
dust collecting
retired but not forgotten
With eyelets missing
torn seams
and lug soles worn so smooth
they appear tired
yet ageless
shining with the memory
of trails they have tread
and camps
at which they've slept

Love II

You have called me back
from the shifting sands
of an undisciplined existence
There I would wander
searching
for something to replace the life
I had once known
fearing each bend in the crooked
often obscured way

Following the drifting call
of your voice
I have returned
to your lush hillsides
And sun warmed valleys
the life of my searching

Though blue skies
and green fields
protect me from the elements
one fear remains
If once again
I fall from grace
as the time must surely come
will I find it hard to leave
or heed your voice again

BOOK IV

Lost Seed

Trainee Guard Duty

The mechanical and effortless pace
leaves your mind free to think of one time since
Halt, port arms, right face, shoulder arms
March on

Glancing the clear and icy sky above
you dwell on moon light, sun light, waves and love
Halt, port arms, right face, shoulder arms
March on

Biting cold dulls the meter-measured pace
Weapon's weight sends pain to your shoulder's base
Halt, port arms, right face, right shoulder arms
March on

Alone in strange, dark and seeming abyss
you remember the life you left for this
Halt, port arms, right face, shoulder arms
March on

The Paratrooper's Second Love

Orders came, I jump tomorrow
So kiss me once before I go

Every jump I fear my fate
Maybe the 'chute opening late

Or landing so my legs might break
This fear I bear for mission sake

But come my love and comfort me
For tempered even steel must be

The River Of Battle

The river lies still
the night crystal clear
The crickets' high-pitched hum is the only sound
The pale yellow moon casts an eerie glow over the lush
tropical foliage

A lone soldier
hesitates in his watch along the pontoon bridge
He removes his helmet
and wipes his forehead dry

A lone soldier
looks at the full moon and starry sky
absorbs the night's beauty
and thinks of life back home

A lone soldier
is shot in the back of the head

Mourning the Man

I've stepped out of life
for a time to morn
the loss of a soldier
dedicated not to war
but to administering aid
to brothers injured
in the cause of their country
His country

He died not alone
Others fell beside him
We salute their souls
with cannon roar
as yet another blast
rocks that battlefield
And the cost of freedom
is paid for

once again

Waiting

As the city rambles on its way
in a yellow haze
noise subdued by sadness
of day's end
the neon signs and signal lights
stand out against buildings graying
in the dusk of failing day
I walk alone among the throng
mind detached
waiting
      for what I cannot say

In The Company Of Solitude

I rested awhile in my labor
sitting on the pile of four-foot lengths
and looked, then, at the blue-gray shadows
of uncut trees fast growing over
                the yellow-orange white
I listened to the breath of winter
cold wind in birch twigs and cedar boughs
hearing around me the quiet hush
pervading the aging day, muted
                 absorbed into snow
I returned to my tiresome task
neither alone nor an intruder
in the company of solitude
I am but one of the family
                hoping to survive

Darkness night

In the dark of night
Naught seems right
Meager lamp glow
Cast more shadow
Than cheerful light
Against the fright

In The Middle Ground

We have come so far from the rock
holding our torches high with pride
We have won battles, bravely fought
over all our natural foe

To gain what
but bloody beaches
fallow fields
and corrupt cadre

Still
our wind-whipped banner points the way
on, to shimmering summit
distant and so far out of reach

So here we stand
upon the middle ground
blocked by righteous ramparts of our own design
in precarious balance, waiting

for the heights to crumble
waiting for the tide

A mid-Winter's Nightmare: a dark and stormy night

In cabin tight
we hunker down
to wait out night
until the dawn

as in the caves
ancestors cowed
in by-gone days
their shoulders bowed

'gainst terrors in
the living night
that awful demon
with dreadful might

The storm did roar
and vent its ire
upon the door
of our poor lair

A sickly flame
on candle stub
lit our domain
a dreary job

That gloom all 'round
bore on our souls
as shadows bound
about the walls

and monsters hid
in corners black
to jump us should
our guard be slack

A banshee's wail
the wind did shout
at logged wall
that held it out

A-swirl the brunt
of tempest vile
like condor's hunt
o're carrion pile

awaits a chance
to swoop down low
its beak a lance
for slicing blow

Within we try
our tortured best
to close an eye
and pray for rest

On sentry stand
the dark night long
my fear in hand
in heart a song

I stoke the fire
against the cold
and turned an ear
to'rd wind so bold

The tree limbs scratched
at window pane
like talons matched
of beast profane

Then came the morn
a feeble gray
so dark, forlorn
as any day

but wind had died
and ghosts took flight
we thus survived
that stormy night

Printed in the United States
By Bookmasters